MW01248448

A Father's Wish

The Story of Jesus and a Little Boy

We are grateful to the following team of authors for their contributions to *God Loves Me*, a Bible story program for young children. This Bible story, one of a series of fifty-two, was written by Patricia L. Nederveld, managing editor for CRC Publications. Suggestions for using this book were developed by Jesslyn DeBoer, a freelance author from Grand Rapids, Michigan. Yvonne Van Ee, an early childhood educator, served as project consultant and wrote *God Loves Me*, the program guide that accompanies this series of Bible storybooks.

Nederveld has served as a consultant to Title I early childhood programs in Colorado. She has extensive experience as a writer, teacher, and consultant for federally funded preschool, kindergarten, and early childhood programs in Colorado, Texas, Michigan, Florida, Missouri, and Washington, using the *High/Scope* Education Research Foundation curriculum. In addition to writing the *Bible Footprints* church curriculum for four- and five-year-olds, Nederveld edited the revised *Threes* curriculum and the first edition of preschool through second grade materials for the *LiFE* curriculum, all published by CRC Publications.

DeBoer has served as a church preschool leader and as coauthor of the preschool-kindergarten materials for the *LiFE* curriculum published by CRC Publications. She has also written K-6 science and health curriculum for Christian Schools International, Grand Rapids, Michigan, and inspirational gift books for Zondervan Publishing House.

Van Ee is a professor and early childhood program advisor in the Education Department at Calvin College, Grand Rapids, Michigan. She has served as curriculum author and consultant for Christian Schools International and wrote the original *Story Hour* organization manual and curriculum materials for fours and fives.

Photo on page 5 and 20: SuperStock.

© 1998 by CRC Publications, 2850 Kalamazoo Ave. SE, Grand Rapids, MI 49560. All rights reserved. With the exception of brief excerpts for review purposes, no part of this book may be reproduced in any manner whatsoever without written permission from the publisher. Printed in the United States of America on recycled paper. ✪ 1-800-333-8300

"God Loves Me" is a registered trademark of CRC Publications.

Library of Congress Cataloging-in-Publication Data

Nederveld, Patricia L., 1944-
     A father's wish: the story of Jesus and a little boy/Patricia
  L. Nederveld.
       p. cm. — (God loves me; bk. 31)
     Summary: Jesus answered a father's wish when he healed
  a little boy. (Based on the miracle told in John 4:43-53.)
  Includes follow-up activities.
    ISBN 1-56212-300-9
    1. Healing of the nobleman's son (Miracle)—Juvenile literature.
  I. Title. II. Series: Nederveld, Patricia L., 1944- God loves me; bk. 31.
  BT367.H45N43   1998
  232.9'55—dc21   97-53313
                                             CIP
                                             AC

10 9 8 7 6 5 4 3 2 1

A Father's Wish
The Story of Jesus and a Little Boy

PATRICIA L. NEDERVELD

ILLUSTRATIONS BY ANGELA JARECKI

CRC Publications
Grand Rapids, Michigan

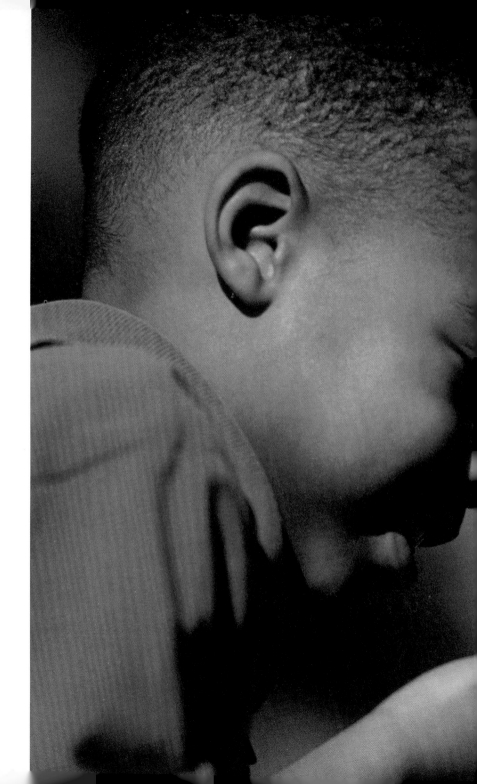

This is a story from God's book, the Bible.

It's for say name(s) of your child(ren). It's for me too!

John 4:43-53

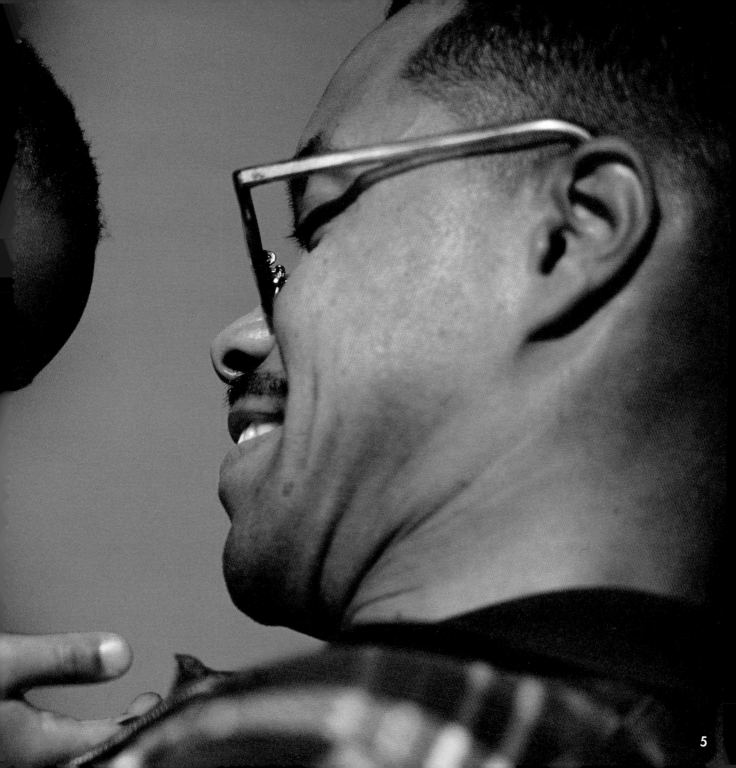

" I love you, my son," said the father each day.

And he smiled at his boy as he ran out to play.

" I love you, my son, but I'm worried today. I can see you feel sick; you need help right away!"

" **I** know what I'll
do—
I know who to
tell—
Jesus! I beg you
to make my son
well!"

"Go back to your home," Jesus said to the man.

"I'll make your son well—you believe that I can!"

Yes, the father believed it, he went on his way.

Then he heard the good news—"Your boy is better today!"

" I love you, my son!" said the dad to his boy. He hugged him and kissed him and smiled with joy.

"Now let us give thanks for what God has done. Jesus has healed you—we believe in God's Son!"

I wonder if you
know that Jesus
can make you
well when you are
sick. . . .

Dear God, thank
you for taking care
of us when we're
sick. We know you
can make us well
again. Amen.

Suggestions for Follow-up

Opening

Cut round Band-Aids into heart shapes. As your little ones arrive today, stick the Band-Aids on their hands and whisper, "God loves you." Look for ways to reassure them that Jesus cares for them when they are sick and can make them well again.

Ahead of time, mount pictures of a mother, father, grandparent, older child, nurse, and doctor on index cards or on construction paper. Spread the pictures out in front of you and invite the children to gather around to play "Name the Helper." Ask the children to point to or name the person or persons who would help them when they fall on the sidewalk and scrape their knees; when they feel sick; when they need medicine; when they need a shot; when they break a bone and need a cast; and so on. Then ask who makes them well when they are sick. Explain that the people in the pictures are *helpers*. They help Jesus take care of us when we are sick or hurt, but Jesus is the one who makes us well.

Learning Through Play

Learning through play is the best way! The following activity suggestions are meant to help you provide props and experiences that will invite the children to play their way into the Scripture story and its simple truth. Try to provide plenty of time for the children to choose their own activities and to play individually. Use group activities sparingly—little ones learn most comfortably with a minimum of structure.

1. Your little ones will enjoy dressing up like medical workers. Provide toy stethoscopes, cotton swabs, craft sticks or tongue depressors, Band-Aids, and strips of cloth for bandages. An old white shirt can be tailored as a lab coat for would-be physicians. Remind your little medical workers that they are Jesus' helpers— they can help Jesus take care of their sick dolls and hurt stuffed animal friends. As you play along, look for opportunities to model your faith in Jesus' compassion and healing powers. Say a prayer of thanks for Jesus' love and care.

2. Set out large blocks and suggest that the children build hospitals and medical clinics. Encourage them to think about how many rooms to build for sick people and where the doctors and nurses will keep their medicine and Band-Aids. Provide toy ambulances and people for them to bring to their hospital. Take advantage of appropriate moments to tell the children that doctors and hospitals are gifts from God to help make us better when we are sick.

3. Stock your art area with the usual paper, glue, and markers, and add tongue depressors, cotton swabs, small Band-Aids, cotton balls, and brown lunch bags. Most young children will simply enjoy experimenting with the texture and shape of these materials. They may want to glue them randomly to paper or to a brown lunch bag to make a doctor's bag. Older children may have fun gluing items to form a pattern or create a new object. As children

work, help them describe the textures and shapes and tell about their creation. Remind them that Jesus can use many people and even things like Band-Aids and tongue depressors to make us well.

4. Sing one or more stanzas of "He's Got the Whole World" (Songs Section, *God Loves Me* program guide). Invite children to mimic these motions:

He's got the whole world . . . (make large circle with arms, cup hands together)
He's got the little tiny baby . . . (rock folded arms as if holding a baby)
He's got everybody here . . . (join hands to form circle)

—Words: African-American spiritual

Closing

Ask your little ones to form a prayer circle. This may be a new experience, so help them follow your directions. Stand, hold hands, and say, "Dear God, thank you for taking care of us. Amen." Then ask if anyone has "owies." Don't be surprised if they all do! Let the children climb into your lap, one at a time. Hug each one, and invite all the children to circle around you as you pray, "Dear God, take care of [name child you're holding]. Amen."

—Adapted from "Praying with Toddlers" Nursery Notes, September/October 1995. Reprinted by permission from *Children's Ministry Magazine*, © 1995, Group Publishing, Box 481, Loveland, CO 80539.

At Home

Make prayers for family members and friends who are sick a regular part of your prayer time, and let your little one sense how much you rely on Jesus to make them well again. Sing, "God cares for [person's name]" to the tune of "God Is So Good." Let your child help you share God's love—you could make a card, a favorite beverage, or a small gift for the person who needs comforting.

Old Testament Stories

Blue and Green and Purple Too! *The Story of God's Colorful World*

It's a Noisy Place! *The Story of the First Creatures*

Adam and Eve *The Story of the First Man and Woman*

Take Good Care of My World! *The Story of Adam and Eve in the Garden*

A Very Sad Day *The Story of Adam and Eve's Disobedience*

A Rainy, Rainy Day *The Story of Noah*

Count the Stars! *The Story of God's Promise to Abraham and Sarah*

A Girl Named Rebekah *The Story of God's Answer to Abraham*

Two Coats for Joseph *The Story of Young Joseph*

Plenty to Eat *The Story of Joseph and His Brothers*

Safe in a Basket *The Story of Baby Moses*

I'll Do It! *The Story of Moses and the Burning Bush*

Safe at Last! *The Story of Moses and the Red Sea*

What Is It? *The Story of Manna in the Desert*

A Tall Wall *The Story of Jericho*

A Baby for Hannah *The Story of an Answered Prayer*

Samuel! Samuel! *The Story of God's Call to Samuel*

Lions and Bears! *The Story of David the Shepherd Boy*

David and the Giant *The Story of David and Goliath*

A Little Jar of Oil *The Story of Elisha and the Widow*

One, Two, Three, Four, Five, Six, Seven! *The Story of Elisha and Naaman*

A Big Fish Story *The Story of Jonah*

Lions, Lions! *The Story of Daniel*

New Testament Stories

Jesus Is Born! *The Story of Christmas*

Good News! *The Story of the Shepherds*

An Amazing Star! *The Story of the Wise Men*

Waiting, Waiting, Waiting! *The Story of Simeon and Anna*

Who Is This Child? *The Story of Jesus in the Temple*

Follow Me! *The Story of Jesus and His Twelve Helpers*

The Greatest Gift *The Story of Jesus and the Woman at the Well*

A Father's Wish *The Story of Jesus and a Little Boy*

Just Believe! *The Story of Jesus and a Little Girl*

Get Up and Walk! *The Story of Jesus and a Man Who Couldn't Walk*

A Little Lunch *The Story of Jesus and a Hungry Crowd*

A Scary Storm *The Story of Jesus and a Stormy Sea*

Thank You, Jesus! *The Story of Jesus and One Thankful Man*

A Wonderful Sight! *The Story of Jesus and a Man Who Couldn't See*

A Better Thing to Do *The Story of Jesus and Mary and Martha*

A Lost Lamb *The Story of the Good Shepherd*

Come to Me! *The Story of Jesus and the Children*

Have a Great Day! *The Story of Jesus and Zacchaeus*

I Love You, Jesus! *The Story of Mary's Gift to Jesus*

Hosanna! *The Story of Palm Sunday*

The Best Day Ever! *The Story of Easter*

Goodbye—for Now *The Story of Jesus' Return to Heaven*

A Prayer for Peter *The Story of Peter in Prison*

Sad Day, Happy Day! *The Story of Peter and Dorcas*

A New Friend *The Story of Paul's Conversion*

Over the Wall *The Story of Paul's Escape in a Basket*

A Song in the Night *The Story of Paul and Silas in Prison*

A Ride in the Night *The Story of Paul's Escape on Horseback*

The Shipwreck *The Story of Paul's Rescue at Sea*

Holiday Stories

Selected stories from the New Testament to help you celebrate the Christian year

Jesus Is Born! *The Story of Christmas*

Good News! *The Story of the Shepherds*

An Amazing Star! *The Story of the Wise Men*

Hosanna! *The Story of Palm Sunday*

The Best Day Ever! *The Story of Easter*

Goodbye—for Now *The Story of Jesus' Return to Heaven*

These fifty-two books are the heart of God Loves Me, a Bible story program designed for young children. Individual books (or the entire set) and the accompanying program guide God Loves Me are available from CRC Publications (1-800-333-8300).